Superstars
of the
BOSTON
RED SOX

by Max Hammer

amicus
high interest

Amicus High Interest is published by Amicus
P.O. Box 1329, Mankato, MN 56002
www.amicuspublishing.us

Library of Congress Cataloging-in-Publication Data
Hammer, Max.
  Superstars of the Boston Red Sox / by Max Hammer.
    pages cm. -- (Pro sports superstars)
  Includes index.
  Summary: "Presents some of the Boston Red Sox's greatest players and
their achievements in pro baseball, including Pedro Martinez, David
Ortiz, and Dustin Pedroia"--Provided by publisher.
  ISBN 978-1-60753-591-1 (hardcover) -- ISBN 978-1-60753-625-3 (pdf
ebook)
  1. Boston Red Sox (Baseball team)--History--Juvenile literature. I. Title.
  GV875.B62H36 2014
  796.357'640974461--dc23
                        2013048646

Photo Credits: Winslow Townson/AP Images, cover; Michael Tureski/Icon
SMI, 2, 21; Elise Amendola/AP Images, 5, 17, 22; Bettmann/Corbis, 7; Ted
Sande/AP Images, 8; Neal Preston/Corbis, 11; Steve Lipofsky/Corbis, 12, 14;
Steven King/Icon SMI, 19

Produced for Amicus by The Peterson Publishing Company
and Red Line Editorial.

Editor Arnold Ringstad
Designer Maggie Villaume
Printed in the United States of America
Mankato, MN
2-2014
PA10001
10 9 8 7 6 5 4 3 2 1

TABLE OF CONTENTS

MEET THE BOSTON RED SOX

The Boston Red Sox have been around since 1901. Since then they have won eight **World Series**. There have been many Boston Red Sox stars. Here are some of the best.

DENTON "CY" YOUNG

Denton "Cy" Young first pitched in 1890. He won 511 games. This included the 1903 World Series. The **Cy Young Award** was named for him. It is given to the best pitchers every season.

Young pitched the most innings ever. His total was 7,355.

7

TED WILLIAMS

Ted Williams was one of the top hitters ever. He had a great **batting average** in 1941. It was .406. No one else has come close since then.

Williams was in the Navy in World War II.

CARL YASTRZEMSKI

Carl Yastrzemski was known as "Yaz." He was a skilled fielder. He was also a great hitter. He won the **Triple Crown** in 1967. Only one other player has won the Triple Crown since then.

JIM RICE

Jim Rice played left field for the Red Sox. He was a strong hitter for many years. In ten of his seasons he hit more than 20 **home runs**. His highest total came in 1978. He hit 46 home runs that year.

WADE BOGGS

Wade Boggs played third base. He got many hits. Boggs won five batting titles. This meant he had the top batting average in the league. The last was in 1988.

Boggs played in the longest game ever. It lasted more than eight hours.

PEDRO MARTINEZ

Pedro Martinez was a great pitcher. He could throw many kinds of pitches. He was Boston's **ace**. Martinez won two Cy Young Awards in Boston. The last was in 2000.

17

DAVID ORTIZ

David Ortiz is a strong hitter. He has the team record for most home runs in a season. He hit 54 in 2006. Ortiz also helped Boston win three World Series.

Ortiz helps raise money for kids in need.

DUSTIN PEDROIA

Dustin Pedroia joined the Red Sox in 2006. He plays second base. Pedroia quickly became a star for his hitting skills. He won an **MVP** award in 2008.

The Red Sox have had many great superstars. Who will be next?

21

TEAM FAST FACTS

Founded: 1901

Other names: Boston Americans (1901–1907)

Nicknames: BoSox, The Sox

Home Stadium: Fenway Park (Boston, Massachusetts)

World Series Championships: 8 (1903, 1912, 1915, 1916, 1918, 2004, 2007, and 2013)

Hall of Fame Players: 34, including Cy Young, Ted Williams, Carl Yastrzemski, and Jim Rice (also 11 managers)

WORDS TO KNOW

ace – the best starting pitcher on a team

batting average – a number that tells how often a player hits the ball

Cy Young Award – an award given to the best pitcher in each league after each season

home runs – hits that go far enough to leave the field, letting the hitter run all the way around the bases to score a run

MVP – Most Valuable Player; an honor given to the best player each season

Triple Crown – when a player leads his league in batting average, home runs, and RBIs in the same season

World Series – the annual baseball championship series

LEARN MORE

Books

Gilbert, Sara. *Boston Red Sox*. Mankato, MN: Creative Education, 2013.

Goodman, Michael E. *The Story of the Boston Red Sox*. Mankato, MN: Creative Education, 2012.

Web Sites

Baseball History
http://mlb.mlb.com/mlb/history/
Learn more about the history of baseball.

Boston Red Sox—Official Site
http://boston.redsox.mlb.com
Watch video clips and read stories about the Boston Red Sox.

MLB.com
http://mlb.com
See pictures and track your favorite baseball player's stats.

INDEX